INTERVIEWING WITH CONFIDENCE

For those who encouraged me to write.

Contents

Introduction	1
Interviewee, Know Thyself	5
Pre-Interview Self-Assessment	7
SWOT Yourself	13
Research. Research? Research!	21
Company Research Guide	25
The Job Description	33
Digging Into the Job Description	34
Connecting Your Experiences to the Job	37
The Resume to Job Description Cross Check	39
Scenario-Based Behavioral Questions	43
Open-Ended Questions	54
Illegal Interview Topics	85
Nonverbal Communication & Professional Presentation	103
Mock Interview Self-Critique	107
Interacting with Interviewers	119
Create Your Questions	122
Wellness Check	123
Final Thoughts	127

INTRODUCTION

Interviews are the type of activity that you get better at with practice. Over time you learn what stories are most effective, which examples fall flat, and how to present yourself most effectively. Unfortunately, most interviewees don't have much time to perfect the craft. Most interviewees want the job search process to be as short and sweet as possible... for obvious reasons! The more you interview, the longer you're not doing the job you want.

Most people I know are terrified of interviewing. Outside of the interview, they are able to articulate why they are qualified and why they want the job. They're practice interview rock stars! But as soon as they get to the real deal, the nerves kick in and it all falls apart. Interviews are high-stress, high-stakes situations, so this is completely normal and happens every day. ... But it doesn't have to happen to you!

I created this workbook to help people get over that interview anxiety hump. Through the chapters that follow, I hope to empower you – the interviewee – with a level of confidence that will carry you through your interview.

A Note on the Content

This workbook is designed to help you prepare for a behavioral interview – one that is used to assess your character traits and personality in relation to a particular job. Many employers use this type of interview if they are not looking for a large amount of technical skills in a particular area. Obviously you need some, and you will likely be asked specific questions about them, but behavioral interviews are more focused on fit than function.

These types of questions are either open-ended or

scenario-based, and we'll go over both kinds later on. Interviewers ask these types of questions to get a sense of how you would respond if presented with a similar situation at their organization. While it may feel weird for you to spend an interview telling stories, this approach makes sense from an employer's perspective: They can train you to do the job but they are trying to determine if they want to. As you may have guessed, your job in an interview is to make them want to.

About the Book

This content started as an interactive ebook of the same name, then became a blog series, and is now this workbook. Through its various iterations, I have updated it to be as useful and easy to use as possible.

There are ten parts, each touching on a different aspect of interview preparation. Every chapter contains an activity designed to help you practice what you just read about. Yes, it's homework... But this is a *workbook*, so you should be expecting to do some work! I promise it's not just to keep you occupied. Each activity should help you get better at interviewing... which is why you bought this thing in the first place!

While this workbook is designed to help you prepare for a specific interview, it is flexible enough for you to use even if you're not at the interviewing stage of your job search. Just do through the activities with your goal job and company in mind!

- In *Chapter 1: Interviewee, Know Thyself,* we'll go into the importance of self-assessment as interview preparation. Then, you'll do some activities that will help you get to know your professional self a bit better.
- In *Chapter 2: Research? Research. Research!,* you will learn the why and how of doing research on the company you're interviewing with. To practice, you will answer detailed questions about a company you're interested in.

- In *Chapter 3: Revisiting the Job Description,* you learn how to mine a job description for exactly what the company is looking for. Then, you will do this with a job you're interested in.
- *Chapter 4: Connecting Your Experiences To The Job* gives you a chance to connect the content of your resume to the job you're prepping to interview for.
- *Chapter 5: Scenario-Based Behavioral Questions* and *Chapter 6: Common Open-Ended Questions* are where we finally get into practicing questions. In the former, you'll learn what scenario-based questions are and a killer strategy for preparing your stories. In the latter, I provide explanations of the most common questions, and tips on how to craft your responses. In each chapter, there is space for you to prepare a response to each question we cover.
- In *Chapter 7: Illegal Interview Questions*, we'll touch on topics that can't legally be asked in interviews, and you'll practice ways for you to avoid sharing content you're uncomfortable with in your interview.
- *Chapter 8: Nonverbal Communication & Professional Presentation* we'll go into the importance of what you don't say, and you'll practice by assessing yourself in a video mock interview.
- In *Chapter 9: Interacting with Your Interviewer(s)*, we'll talk about the importance of asking questions at the end of your interview, also the why and how of thank you notes.
- *Chapter 10: Wellness Check*, the final chapter of Interviewing With Confidence, I'll give you some tips on maintaining your job-search sanity.

The Interviewing Mindset
As you move through the book, keep this in mind:
    If a company is taking the time and energy to interview

you, chances are really good that they are interested in hiring you. Most businesses don't reach out to even a quarter of the people who apply to their jobs because of the sheer amount of resources that interviewing requires. If they call you they, at the very least, like your application and are willing to see if you match it.

This is great to remember because it means you shouldn't spend your prep time worrying about how to sell your qualifications for the job. The company knows them and thinks you have enough of them to do their job. Your interview should be a time where you let them get to know you. Yes, discuss the specifics of why you should be hired, but that should not be your focus. They already like you, so get them to want to hire you.

This book will show you how.

CHAPTER 1
INTERVIEWEE, KNOW THYSELF

Self-knowledge is the key to all aspects of the job search and any subsequent career development. After all, how can you know that you're on the right track if you have no idea where you want to go? In this chapter, we'll go over why knowing yourself is a critical aspect of a successful interview. Then, in the related activities, you'll have to chance to dig deeper into your past and mine your past experiences for stories you can tell to your interviewer.

I'm starting out this workbook with the importance of knowing yourself because it is the first step towards interviewing with confidence. Interviews are often the first and only chance to impress a potential employer enough for them to want to hire you. While they may have a sense of your qualifications from your application documents, how you present them is critical in helping your interviewers connect the dots between you and the job.

Having a deep understanding of who you are and what you bring to the position will help you in an interview because you will be able to more easily convey these things to the interviewer. You won't have to stumble through anything because you'll be prepared to pull out the most relevant aspects of your background.

On the flipside, knowing your shortfalls will make you better able to craft responses that counteract the points that could detract from your candidacy. You know you'll get questions about what you need to work on, so having this information handy will make it less likely for you to be tripped up. (Which is often the case with the 'perceived negative' questions that ask about weaknesses and the like.)

In short, it is equally important to know who you are and who you are not.

Having this meta-level knowledge – both generally and as it relates to the position you're interviewing for – is more helpful than memorizing a bunch of responses to interview questions that may or may not be asked. That's how most people prepare for interviews, and it makes the process much more stressful. Even if the interviewer asks you the exact questions that you've memorized responses for (which is rare), the chances of you responding like a rehearsed robot are huge. This is not good.

You need to know yourself and your experiences well enough to be able to answer whatever questions come your way. By deeply interrogating your past for highlights to share and low lights to explain away, you won't be caught off guard in a stressful interview situation.

Caveat: I'm not saying that you shouldn't prepare any of your responses - it's just as bad when folks try to wing it in an interview. But you need to prep the right way, and memorization is not the right way! (Don't worry! We'll go over this elusive "right way" later on.)

NOW PRACTICE!

The self-assessment activities for this first chapter will get you thinking about key details about your past experiences that you may want to highlight in an interview. Answer the questions honestly so that you can get the best, most accurate, results.

PRE-INTERVIEW SELF-ASSESSMENT

Leadership Skills and Experiences

Write about the last two instances where you help a leadership role, and make note of the following:
- How you got the role
- How many people you were charged with leading
- One challenge you faced
- One task you accomplished
- One lesson you learned

_____
_____
_____
_____
_____
_____
_____
_____
_____
_____
_____
_____
_____
_____
_____
_____
_____
_____

Write down at least two situations where you displayed leadership skills but were not in an official leadership role. For each instance, make note of the following:
- The situation or circumstance that made you take on that role
- How others reacted to your display of leadership
- One lesson you learned
- Something you would do differently if presented with this situation in the future

_____
_____
_____
_____
_____
_____
_____
_____
_____
_____
_____
_____
_____
_____
_____
_____
_____
_____

Teamwork Skills and Experiences

Write down two instances where you displayed teamwork. Think about the when and where, then make note of the challenges and accomplishments involved in each experience. Try to make sure your examples come from a variety of experiences to ensure that you don't repeat yourself too much in your interview.

What role do you tend to take on a team? Why?

Where are you strongest and weakest on a team? How are you working to address the weak parts?

What is your general approach and outlook when asked to work in a team? How did you develop this view?

_____
_____
_____
_____
_____
_____
_____
_____
_____
_____

Communication Styles and Skills

What is your communication style? Where and how did you develop it?

_____
_____
_____
_____
_____
_____
_____
_____
_____
_____
_____

When have you had to change your communication style for a specific audience?

_____
_____
_____
_____
_____
_____
_____
_____
_____
_____
_____
_____
_____
_____

Problem Solving Skills

On a scale of 1 to 4, rate yourself on the following:

_____	Identifying problems
_____	Anticipating problems
_____	Critically thinking though an issue
_____	Researching, fact-finding, and fact-checking

_____	Developing solutions
_____	Implementing solutions
_____	Assessing and evaluating your own work
_____	Implementing lessons learned

Pick two of the highest ranked qualities from the previous activity and write down stories surrounding your experiences using them

_____
_____
_____
_____
_____
_____
_____
_____
_____
_____
_____
_____
_____
_____
_____
_____
_____
_____
_____
_____

Pick two of the lowest ranked qualities from the prior activity and write out ways to improve in these areas.

_____
_____
_____
_____
_____
_____
_____
_____
_____
_____
_____
_____
_____
_____
_____
_____
_____
_____
_____
_____
_____

SWOT YOURSELF

This activity will help you synthesize your strengths, weaknesses, opportunities, and threats. In the space provided, write out responses to the related prompts.

Strengths

What are you good at?
What skill sets and professional qualities do you bring to this job? To this company?
What strengths do others see in you?
What other strengths do you see in yourself?

_____
_____
_____
_____
_____
_____
_____
_____
_____
_____
_____
_____
_____
_____
_____
_____
_____
_____
_____
_____
_____
_____
_____
_____

Weaknesses

What skills and professional qualities do you need to work on?
What skills, qualities, and/or resources are you lacking?
What traits do you have that could post a problem in this position? To this company?
What do others think you need to work on?

_____
_____
_____
_____
_____
_____
_____
_____
_____
_____
_____
_____
_____
_____
_____
_____
_____
_____
_____
_____
_____
_____
_____
_____
_____
_____
_____
_____

Opportunities

What professional opportunities are open to you?
How can you turn your weaknesses into opportunities?
How can you turn your strengths into opportunities?
What opportunities do you have to expand upon your strengths?
How can you create more opportunities for yourself?

_____
_____
_____
_____
_____
_____
_____
_____
_____
_____
_____
_____
_____
_____
_____
_____
_____
_____
_____
_____

Threats

What industry trends could harm you careers?
What barriers and/or obstacles do you face in your current career path?
Who or what is your main competition?
Are any of your weaknesses also threats?
Could any of your strengths or opportunities become threats?

_____
_____
_____
_____
_____
_____
_____
_____
_____
_____
_____
_____
_____
_____
_____
_____
_____
_____
_____
_____

Now reflect!

What did you learn from this activity?
How do you think it will be useful in your interview?

CHAPTER 2
RESEARCH. RESEARCH? RESEARCH!

In the last chapter, I stressed the importance of self-knowledge. This time, we're moving on to company knowledge: why it's important and how to get it. In this chapter, we'll go through the ways that you can research companies in preparation for your interviews. Then, you'll practice these tips by actually researching a company that you're interested in.

Thorough company research is important for a few reasons. First, and most obviously, the interviewers will expect you to know details about their company that are beyond what they state in the job description. Iterations of the 'Why us' question are very common across industries, so it's very helpful to have an informed, well-researched (and accurate!) response to that question. Vague answers like 'You're the best in your field' won't cut it, especially in later interview rounds. You've got to show them that 1) understand who they are, 2) can add value to what they're doing/trying to do, and 3) want to work for them based on this information.

Doing company research will also help you get a sense of the type of person who would be successful within the organization. This information can help you craft your answers to questions in a way that shows how well you'll fit within their culture, values, mission, and ideals. For example, you don't want to harp too much on your preference for autonomy when the company you're interviewing for prides itself in promoting teamwork and collaboration! Details like this separate the prepared from the unprepared... and the hired from the still seeking.

Of course, the flipside of this is that you could discover information that gives you pause about working for the company. It is way better to find these things out *before* you start working for them, so be on the look out for any details that make you uneasy.

Finally, your company research will help you come up with intelligent questions to ask during the interview. Such questions are critical to showing your interest in both the job and the company. And, as we'll cover later, you never want to ask things that have obvious answers. The Q&A period is also a place for you to ask about anything you found that would make you not want to work for the company. Remember, interviews are as much about them evaluating you as you evaluating them. Use the in-person time wisely.

When conducting company research, pull out things that you like and find unique about the organization, as well as things that you would like more information on. In addition, make note of places that you feel your skill set can contribute the most. These facts will come in handy when you are interviewing, as you will be able to drop them into responses and/or ask deeper questions about them to your interviewers.

How to Research Companies

Company-created info.
The information that the company produces and disseminates is incredibly useful in understanding how it sees itself in the broader landscape of the industry that it's in. In addition, it has content that will give you insight into what they deem most important about themselves. To link it to interviewing, it's the company version of the "Tell me about yourself" question. Study the organization's website – particularly the parts most relevant to what you're

being interviewed for (departments, initiatives, etc.) – and take notes. Are there specific projects or programs that they're touting? What are their stated goals and values? What else do they harp on? This is the information that will show that you are an informed interviewee.

Company-related info.
Use the internet to figure out what the company is currently getting press for. Is it positive? Negative? Related to the department you've applied to? Depending on how much lead time you have between the invitation to interview and when you actually do it, it might be helpful to set up Google alerts to be sent to you whenever they are in the news. In some industries (like financial services), interview questions about company activity and up-to-the-day information like stock prices and public deals are standard. Having this data delivered to you could prove critical to your success.

Know their place.
In addition to knowing what the specific company is up to, you should also look into their competitors and their place in the industry as a whole. Figure out:

- Are they the establishment that sets the status quo, an upstart looking to change the game, or a Steady Eddie content with where they are?
- Who else does the same work? What are the similarities and differences between this company and others who occupy similar spaces?
- What are popular opinions about this company? Are they positive or negative? How have they changed over time?

This information will be useful in helping you discuss what sets this company apart from the rest, and for giving your interviewers concrete reasons for your desire to join their team.

Researching Interviewers.

If you are told who your interviewers will be, you should definitely research them. Use their company bio, LinkedIn profile, and other public information to get a better sense of who will be evaluating you. Sometimes it's nice to know if you will have things in common with them, like schools or hobbies. This way, you can sprinkle your commonalities into your responses to their questions and build some major bridges.

Even if there isn't anything in common, use any insights you gain to humanize the interviewers. Remember: An interview is just a conversation.

NOW PRACTICE!

Use the following activity to research the company that you're planning to interview with. If you're not preparing for something specific, look up your dream company and do the activity with them in mind.

COMPANY RESEARCH GUIDE

Who runs the company? How long have they been there?

_____
_____
_____
_____
_____
_____

What is the company's mission? What are their values?

_____
_____
_____
_____
_____
_____

How do you see yourself contributing to the company's goals?

_____
_____
_____
_____
_____
_____
_____

Where does the position you're interviewing for fit into the larger organizational structure of the company?

___

What are some of the department's goals or current initiatives?

___

Name at least two of the company's competitors.

___

What are the key similarities and differences between the competitors and the company you're interviewing with?

___

What do you like best about the company?

___

What do you dislike the most about the company? If hired, how will you get over these misgivings?

___

What are some potential challenges you would face if hired?

_____
_____
_____
_____
_____
_____
_____

Where could you add value to the company?

_____
_____
_____
_____
_____
_____
_____

What more do you want to know about the company? The position?

_____
_____
_____
_____
_____
_____
_____

Find anything else noteworthy? Write it here!

CHAPTER 3
THE JOB DESCRIPTION

In this chapter, we'll go into the importance of the job description and how it is an invaluable tool for interview preparation. Then, you'll practice by digging into the job description of the interview you're preparing for.

Most people apply to jobs and never look at the job description again. They just hit 'submit' and move on to the next one. Big mistake! Job descriptions contain a wealth of information on both the company and the candidate whom they would prefer to hire. These descriptions often tip savvy applicants off to what the company is looking for the most by repeating words, phrases, and activities. As such, you can use it to tailor your preparation and figure out which specific aspects of the position you want to highlight in your interview.

But don't worry! You don't have to speak to *everything* a company asks for. Often, job descriptions are a wish list for employers. If they can find some magic person who fits all of their qualifications, great! But they know that the likelihood of this is very slim. Therefore, you should figure out the ones that resonate most with your experiences and focus on those. If the job description asks for eight things and you know you can do five, concentrate your preparation on helping the interviewers know that you'd crush it at that job because of those 5 things.

On the flipside, you also need to know exactly where your experiences miss the mark and be prepared to explain how you will pick up the skills that you're missing. Knowing this will show the interviewer that 1) you're self-aware enough to know that you're not perfect and 2) you've thought about to how to bring yourself up to speed. This is an assurance that you will actually follow through if hired. Bonus points if you're already trying to improve your relevant skill set. (Pro tip: Any skill that falls into this 'working on it' category is great for a "What is your greatest weakness?" response!)

On a more obvious level, you need to dig into the job description because you'll be asked directly about the tasks and responsibilities outlined in it. You have to remember them and communicate your previous experiences will them or else the interviewer will think that you don't know what you're interviewing for. Interviewers (like most people) hate feeling like their time is being wasted, and this is something they do not forget.

NOW PRACTICE!

Go back to the posting for the job you're preparing to interview for (or one that you'd like to interview for) and answer the prompts below.

DIGGING INTO THE JOB DESCRIPTION

Why did you apply to this position?

_____
_____
_____
_____
_____
_____
_____

What initially piqued your interest?

_____
_____
_____
_____
_____
_____

What are the strongest places of fit between yourself and the position?

_____
_____
_____
_____
_____
_____

What are the strongest places of disconnect between yourself and the position?

_____
_____
_____
_____
_____
_____

Now research the job title to see what people in this position typically do. You can do this with a simple Google search, a keyword search in a job search engine (such as Indeed.com), or on a website like the Bureau of Labor Statistics (bls.gov). When you've gathered more information, answer the following questions.

What are the similarities between the job and what you found in your research?

_____
_____
_____
_____
_____
_____
_____
_____

What are the differences between the job and what you found in your research?

_____
_____
_____
_____
_____
_____
_____
_____

Why do you think this role is different within this particular company? (Use your previous research to answer this one!)

_____
_____
_____
_____
_____
_____
_____
_____
_____

Other notes

_____
_____
_____
_____
_____
_____
_____
_____
_____
_____
_____
_____
_____

CHAPTER 4
CONNECTING YOUR EXPERIENCES TO THE JOB

In this chapter, we'll discuss why you need to think beyond your resume bullet points so that you can convey rich details to your interviewer. In the activity, you will connect your resume to the job description you used in the previous activity.

Know More Than Your Resume

It goes without saying that you need to know the content of your resume in order to have a successful interview. The ability to answer the 'whats' and 'whys' of your previous professional experiences are crucial to obtaining new ones. In addition, you have to know more than your resume so that you can provide context to the one-pager. *Prove that you're more than a piece of paper!*

Start by thinking critically about each experience that is on your resume in terms of results and accomplishments (as opposed to tasks and responsibilities.) How did you change from the experience? What has hindsight taught you? With such insights, you can show the interviewer what you actually did instead of just telling them what you were supposed to do. This gives the interviewer a sense of your career trajectory and provides evidence of professional growth. (Both good things!)

Understanding what parts of your resume are most relevant to the position you're being interviewed for is the goal of fleshing out your experiences since these are things you will probably be asked about the most. Think of it like a Venn diagram: What are the points of overlap between what you've done and the job you're going for? This is where the job description comes in handy! Revisiting it is a great start for this since, as discussed in the previous chapter, it probably contains a wealth of information about whom the company is looking to hire.

In addition to the actual position posting (or in case the posting is not descriptive), research what else the job entails by reading the company website, asking people who work there (hint: find them on LinkedIn!), and looking the websites that you used in the previous chapter's activities. Such information will provide insight into the typical tasks and responsibilities of such a position, and help you color in the details of the one you're about to interview for. Once you have this list, you can go back to your resume and begin to craft stories that highlight the places where your past connects to the position.

NOW PRACTICE!

In the following activity, you will think critically about where your experiences fit with the job you used in the previous chapter. Remember: The only way this is useful is if it's real, so be honest!

THE RESUME TO JOB DESCRIPTION CROSS CHECK

Step 1: Read your resume and the job description closely.

Step 2: Write down as many places of overlap between the two documents.

Step 3: Read both documents again. Then write out any points of overlap that you missed in the first go. Then, write out the places where you see a lack of fit between your resume and the job description.

Step 4: Answer the following questions.

What are three skills, qualifications, and/or experiences that you think fit best between your resume and the job description?

_____
_____
_____
_____
_____
_____
_____
_____
_____
_____

What are two resume items that are unlikely heroes – things you see as strengths but might need to be explained?

_____
_____
_____
_____
_____
_____
_____
_____
_____
_____

What are two places where you are sorely lacking in skills, qualifications, and/or experience?

___

___

___

___

___

___

___

___

___

___

Brainstorm ways to explain these items away in an interview.

___

___

___

___

___

___

___

___

___

___

___

___

CHAPTER 5
SCENARIO-BASED BEHAVIORAL QUESTIONS

Now that you've done some self-assessment and research, it's time to delve into actual interview questions. This chapter deals with behavioral questions, while the next one digs into the common open-ended ones. The prompts below will walk you through the steps to crafting a complete response to these types of questions, and provides space for you to construct your own responses.

Scenario-based behavioral interview questions ask the interviewee to describe a scenario to illustrate a particular circumstance. They tend to start out with phrases like "Tell me about a time when" or "Describe a time where". These questions can be tricky if you aren't prepared, so you should aim to have 5-7 stories or situations prepped for each interview. Keyword is prepped, not memorized! So how should you do this? With CARL!

The CARL method is great for behavioral interview questions because it helps you structure a story that is a complete, start-to-finish narrative.

CARL stands for: Context, Action, Result, Lesson

- *Context* - What was the situation or presenting problem? Where did it take place? (This piece sets the scene for the story that you're about to tell.)
- *Action* - What did you do? What was your response to the situation or presenting problem described in the 'context'?
- *Result* - What was the outcome of your action? How did the immediate situation resolve?
- *Lesson* - What did you learn from this situation? How

would you apply what you learned to future situations?

Lesson is perhaps the most important part of this method because it gives the interviewer insight into how you would respond if presented with the situation again. Unfortunately, in my experience with interviewing (both mock and real), this is the part that is usually missing from more inexperienced interviewees. You must end your stories with evidence that you learned from your experience or else your response will be incomplete.

What this looks like in real life
Imagine yourself in an interview. The interviewer says: *Tell me about a time you implemented a solution to a workplace problem.*

The planning:

- *Context:* Boss' desire to engage with clients who had purchased from our company in the past
- *Action:* Created and implemented a digital media strategy
- *Result:* Increased customer engagement with the store, both in-person and online
- *Lesson:* I can use my skillset to add value to my company

The response:

[C] My company was looking for new ways to engage with previous customers, and my boss decided that we should explore online avenues to do so. She asked me to investigate and come up with a plan. [A] Since I have both personal and professional experience with online media, I created a strategy for the company to follow. In it, I proposed we send out regular email campaigns along with cultivating a stronger social media presence. *[R]* After adopting and implementing these initiatives 3 months ago, my company has experienced a 25% increase in customer engagement and made over $100,000 from repeat business. *[L]* From this experience, I learned that I can utilize my skill set to add value to the company and create a more positive customer experience. I plan to continue to hone these skills so that I can contribute to whatever future opportunities arise.

Remember: You can use the job description to get an idea of what types of behavioral questions to prepare for. For example, if it mentions working in a team, then it is safe to assume that you will be asked about your experiences in such settings. When preparing for an interview, it is a great idea to pull out these types of cues and prep stories that go with them first. This way, you know you have the obvious ones covered. And trust me, interviewers know what types of things are obvious and what will be a curveball. It's always a good idea to nail the easy ones!

NOW PRACTICE!

Below are some very common behavioral questions plus the logic behind them. After reading the prompt, use the space below it to construct your answer. It doesn't have to be as pulled together as the example above. It's way easier to recall talking points, so focus on creating ones that convey the information that you'd like the interviewer to know.

Tell me about a time you successfully worked on a team.

Employers love interpersonal skills like teamwork, but will rarely train new employees to gain them. Therefore, they ask questions like this one to see how the interviewee has dealt with team projects in the past. When coming up with a response to this, you want to talk more about your interactions than about the project itself. I've seen many instances where respondents get bogged down with providing irrelevant details about what the team was working on rather than discussing their work within the team. Provide just enough details for the interviewers to know what you were doing, but remember that they don't care about that part! They want to know about how you interact with others, so give them that.

Describe a situation where you dealt with a difficult personality.

No workplace is rainbows and sunshine all the time, and employers want to make sure that you can deal with it. Providing them with an example of how you've dealt with a difficult personality in the past is useful in 1) highlighting interpersonal skills and 2) showing how you've learned and grown from the situation. In thinking through your response, don't get caught up with trying to paint yourself in a positive light. Playing the victim isn't the best angle for this one, as you need to be an adult and take ownership of your actions. Honesty and growth are the keys to effectively answer this question.

Tell me about a time you solved a complex problem.

Employers want to know about your problem-solving skills because chances are huge that you'll have to do that in their position. This question could be tricky because your response could highlight other aspects of your work style and interpersonal habits. In preparing for this response, use your research and make sure you're hitting on something that the company values. For example, if they're a deadline-driven environment, it would help your case if you provide details on a time-sensitive situation. As far as behavioral questions go this one is super flexible, so use it to sell yourself in other areas as well.

Describe a significant personal victory.

Personal victories are always fun to share because they allow the interviewers to see a more human side of you. Just as "Tell me about yourself" (which we'll discuss in the next chapter) gives you a chance to provide insight into who you are outside of your resume, this question let you do this within a more specific context. While you have some freedom with this, it's always helpful to connect your victory with something professional – bonus points if it's related to the job you're interviewing for.

Tell me about a time you overcame a professional obstacle.

Employers like to know about a time when you overcame a professional obstacle because, like the question above, it gives them an idea about your character. By showing that you persevered through a difficult experience at work *and* providing examples of how you got through it, you can show that you're able to get through whatever obstacles that could face you in the position you're interviewing for. The key to answering this question is to make sure that 1) it's a professional obstacle (as opposed to a personal one) and 2) you focus on the soft skills you used to overcome it.

Tell me about a time you were the leader of a team.

Leadership experiences are important to many employers because they illustrate a number of soft skills that are important to success on the job. For example: If you're the type of leader who delegates work based on the team members' strengths, then chances are good that you're the type of coworker who builds up those around you. On the contrary, if your leadership style is 'my way or the highway', then a potential employer may assume that you're not the easiest person to work with. As such, you should be prepared to highlight the aspects of your leadership experiences that positively illustrate how you work with others.

Discuss a time you kept calm under pressure.
Similar to the *dealing with a difficult personality* question, this one helps interviewers understand how you handle tough situations. The unsaid part of this question is "at work", so don't use personal examples with friends and family. That could get messy, and make you look petty. Instead, use instances where you had to stay calm in a professional setting. In addition, provide details on the strategies you used and how you dealt with it afterwards.

Tell me about a time you didn't perform to your standards.
Questions about failures and shortcomings are very common in interviews. This is not because employers have some morbid fascination with making interviewees speak negatively about themselves. Rather, responses to questions like this provide valuable information on how an individual understands their mistakes. As such, your response not only needs to illustrate the situation that caused you to fail but also provide insight into what you learned from it. You have to show the interviewers that, if presented with a similar set of circumstances, you wouldn't fail again.

Tell me about a time you had a conflict with your supervisor.

Employers ask questions like this because they want to know your conflict resolution skills and strategies. Like the leadership question above, this one give the interviewers insight into the type of employee and coworker you have been in the past. Since they use these answers to try to figure out the type of employee and coworker you might be in their company, be sure to provide evidence of growth and maturity in your response to a question like this. Even if you didn't handle the conflict in a particularly professional manner, be sure to mention what you learned from the experience and how you would handle yourself differently in the future.

CHAPTER 6
OPEN-ENDED QUESTIONS

In the previous chapter, we did a deep dive into behavioral-based interview questions. In this one, we'll talk about open-ended questions. Just like before, there is space for you to write out an answer after each question, so you can work as you read. As with the rest of the activities in this workbook, try to craft your answers with a specific job in mind.

In addition to job-specific questions, there are questions that you will likely encounter in any interview regardless of the position or industry. Below, I discuss the rationale for these questions and how to approach answering them. Some of the explanations are longer than others because some questions are more complicated than others. Still, I try to give enough of a prompt for each one so that you can develop a proper response in an interview.

Below each prompt, I provide plenty of space for you to brainstorm your own responses. There are a lot of lines because I want you to jot notes and possibilities before you get to the more concise, interview-ready responses.

Tell me about yourself.

You'll get a version of this question in every interview you ever go on, so it's good to have a strategy for it. This question tends to trip people up because it's so open-ended that you could really take it anywhere. But you shouldn't. The strategy for this question is to keep it your response in relation to the job you're interviewing for. (In fact, I tell clients to mentally add "in relation to this job" to the end of that question, just so that they get into the right mindset to answer it.)

How to respond: Think about your past in relation to your present - How did you come to interview for that particular job at that particular company? Tell the interviewer about your first experiences with the field or industry - What piqued your interest? Who influenced you? This question should humanize you, so personal details are not off limits. For example, if you want to be a lawyer because your mom is a lawyer, this is useful information to share. Even if you want to be a lawyer because you were inspired by Elle Woods in *Legally Blonde*, share that, too... It's real! In either case, back it up with examples of how you've done your own information gathering about the field. This shows that your decision to enter the field is an informed on - with it the entire point of this question!

How to screw this up: Unsuccessful respondents tend to fall in the two extremes: too autobiographical or purely professional. It's okay to have personal details but if you start talking about the dog you had when you were five, stop. That's way too much information! On the flipside, it's not enough to give information related to school and work. Don't list out everything on your resume because they know your resume! Instead, provide personal context to your professional experiences and show the interviewer who you really are.

_____
_____
_____
_____
_____
_____
_____
_____

Walk me through your resume.

With this question, interviewers are looking to see how you frame your experiences because it gives them insight on how you think your background fits with their opening. If you highlight irrelevant parts of your resume, for example, then they may get the sense that you don't know what you're interviewing for, then not hire you. While you can point out especially meaningful experiences, keep this to a minimum if they're otherwise irrelevant.

How to respond: First, go in the order of your resume so that it's easier for the interviewer to follow. Second, be sure to highlight the most relevant aspects of your experiences. It's okay to skip over things that don't matter because, like I said before, these details are not important. (FYI: This should be how your resume is constructed anyway.) The flipside of this is if there are any background details or stories that you didn't have space to share on your resume or in your cover letter, you should definitely tell them. For example, if you are interviewing for a marketing job and you didn't have space to detail a marketing plan you made for a previous experience, use this time to talk about it.

How to screw this up: The most important thing to remember is ABP: always be positive. You don't want to speak disparagingly about an experience. If it's that bad or that disconnected from what you're currently pursuing, then don't put in on your resume! Or just gloss over it with a comment about how it 'showed you what you didn't want to do' and keep it moving.

Speaking of keeping it moving: the responses to this question have the potential to be insanely long, so be sure to be as concise as possible. For a 1-page resume, 3 minutes tops. Finally, it's not story time so don't read your resume word-for-word! This is the quickest way to create a disengaged interviewer and cost yourself a job.

Why do you want to work for our company?

This is one of the questions that consistently trips my clients up because people tend to be more concerned about the job they are applying to. I get it – it's called a job search not a company search. But you have to consider the company because that's going to determine how and the conditions under which your job is done. All companies have different cultures, values, professional development opportunities, and priorities. It is up to you to know how the one that you're interviewing for operates. You can get this information from the research you did prior to the interview. (See, this is why you need it!)

How to respond: To successfully answer this question, you need to 1) be able to articulate the unique aspects of the company that set them apart from their competitors, and 2) show that you fit with the way they operate. Highlight the places where your skills and experiences would contribute to what they already do or what they are working on.

How to screw this up: 1) You don't have an answer. Always have an answer! 2) You give a vague one that makes it clear that didn't do your research. 3) You highlight aspects of the company that have nothing to do with the position you're interviewing for. All of these responses show a lack of preparedness for the interview, and a general disregard for the position and company as a whole. Applicants who display these characteristics are highly unlikely to get an offer.

___
___
___
___
___
___

What is your greatest weakness?

This is everyone's least favorite question, and for good reason - it's hard! Interviews put people in the mindset of selling themselves and spinning everything positively, and this question asks you to do the opposite... At least, on the surface. In reality, the interviewer wants to know how you're working to address whatever you think is a professional flaw.

How to respond: Just like in the "Tell me about yourself" question, this question's unsaid part is 'in relation to this job.' Which of your weaknesses would make this particular position challenging to perform? This is where you need to be strategic, as your weakness should not be an essential function of the job. If it is, then you're probably applying for the wrong thing! Think about the weaknesses that you're willing to talk about, and cross-reference them with the job description. This process should help you figure out which one(s) to avoid if asked this tricky question.

This question also has another unsaid part - 'And how are you working on it?' This is the part that most people forget, and why this question is perceived as a way to make applicants speak negatively about themselves. If you just float a flaw out there without addressing what you're doing to fix it, the interviewer will be left with a bad taste in their mouth because it looks like you're okay with the flaw since you're not doing anything about it. Be sure to talk about the steps you're taking to turn the weakness into a strength, and reassure the interviewer that it won't be an issue on the job.

How to screw this up: I already discussed two wrong ways to answer this question: 1) not giving corrective steps, and 2) giving a weakness that is directly related to a key function of the job. A third is to say that you don't have any weaknesses or "Can't think of anything right now." Umm, no. Never say that you don't have any weaknesses. It makes you look like you're full of yourself, which is definitely a weakness.

Why should you be hired?

This question is typically the last one that interviewers ask, so it represents your last chance to sell your qualifications for the position. While you've (hopefully) done this throughout the rest of the interview, now is the time to highlight the key points and leave the interviewer with no doubts.

How to respond: When preparing your response to this question, it is helpful to revisit the job description and whatever research notes you took to ensure you're focused on the right things. (Good thing you have this workbook!) Think about the strongest points that you can mention in your recap, and write them down so that you don't forget while you're under the stress of the interview. Stick to 3-5, so that you don't find yourself giving a monologue at the end of the interview.

How to screw this up: If you feel that you're missing something, don't use your time to apologize for not have certain qualifications. Don't remind the interviewers of your shortcomings, as this is not the last message you want them to receive. Rather, play up the strengths that you have in relation to the position, and emphasize your ability to learn quickly.

_____
_____
_____
_____
_____
_____
_____
_____
_____
_____
_____
_____
_____

Where do you see yourself in 5-10 years?

This question is often asked to entry-level and early career professionals, and is used by interviewers to 1) get a sense of where you want your career to go and 2) see if your desired trajectory fits with where the company is going/hoping to go. This is one of the freer questions, as you don't have to necessarily tailor it to the company. Having a solid, thought out response that shows how the position you're interviewing for fits with your overall plan is the key to this response.

How to respond: Keep in mind - If your ultimate goals are (or could seem) totally different from the position, it might signal to the interviewer that you wouldn't plan to stay very long in you get hired. If your ultimate goals are unrelated (and it's okay if they are), be sure to discuss your timeline and how you see the position contributing to your goals. I've been in situations where a simple explanation to connect the dots goes a very long way.

How to screw this up: Not having a plan or saying that you see yourself in the position you are interviewing for are both ways to mess this one up. Even if your plan isn't 100% fleshed out, you have to show that you're thinking long-term about your career and taking your future seriously. Saying that you want to still be in that same position sounds bad because very few people stay in the same spot for that long. Same company, yes. Same job, no. Both of these responses send the same message to the interviewer: You don't know what you want. And, if you don't know what you want, you probably don't really want this job.

_____
_____
_____
_____
_____
_____
_____
_____
_____
_____
_____
_____

What did you learn from your last job?

In my opinion, there is no such thing as a dead-end job. You should be able to learn something from every employment experience, regardless of the prestige or relevance of the position. Employers like to hear about what you gained from a previous job because they want to know how you take advantage of professional development, even if it's not given by the organization.

How to respond: Now, professional development is a very

fluid term. The conventional definition is that it is training or activities that help you do your job better, but it can be anything that helps you decide the type of professional that you want to be. In the same way that taking an Excel training course can be useful, learning that you work better in a deadline-oriented environment is just as valid in developing you as a professional. When crafting your response, think of a more holistic definition of on the job learning and development and provide an answer that illustrates how you take advantage of all opportunities presented to you.

How to screw this up: You never want to say that you learned nothing from a job. Even if you were given training that you think is relevant to your career, you still learned something. (In this case, you may have learned that you want to work somewhere that provides such training!) You may have to dig deep and get creative, but always provide your interviewer with a nugget that you've learned.

What past experiences most qualify you for this role?

Chances are good that if you're being interviewed for a job, the employer believes that you're qualified to do it. Otherwise, they wouldn't waste the resources to interview you. An employer's desire to see why you think you're qualified stems from their want to hear it from you. They want to see if your explanation of your qualifications differs from theirs.

How to respond: Your response could either confirm their ideas of you or raise questions as to your motivations for applying to their job, so you need to be strategic. With whatever experiences you choose, include any off-the-resume details that are particularly relevant to the job. Dig deep into your reasoning, so that even if it's different than the interviewers' ideas, it works to contribute to their beliefs about your qualifications as opposed to detracts from them.

How to screw up: Since you can't read the interviewers' mind, it's hard to know if your answers will coincide with their ideas. As long as you back up your assertions with solid examples, you should be okay.

_____
_____
_____
_____
_____
_____
_____
_____
_____
_____

How will this job help you achieve your ultimate career goals?

This question asks you to situate the job you're interviewing for within the context of your desired career path. Think of it as a more specific way to ask 'Where do you see yourself in 5-10 years', as the employer wants to get a better idea of where you think this job would fit in your trajectory.

How to respond: For this one, you want to convey how this job will be critical to your development as a professional in your field. Give specific examples of what you hope to learn, and how you plan to leverage these lessons moving forward. In addition, say why the company is the best place for you to be at that given point in your career. This is especially good to say if the job is one that you could do anywhere.

How to screw this up: 1) Saying that you don't know how this job will help you in the future. Even if you don't *really* know, say something! Have a solid response so that the employer doesn't think that you're just taking the job to take it and will leave in a few months. 2) Saying that you don't have an ultimate career goal. It's totally okay if you don't know exactly where you want to be in the future, but don't say this in an interview. Just pick something and go with it for the sake of the interview, especially if you're genuinely interested in the job you're interviewing for.

_____

_____

_____

_____

_____

_____

_____

Why this field or career?

Employers ask this question to gain insight into the interviewee's motivations for applying to their position that go beyond the position itself. This information is useful because it can shed light on the applicant's current motivations and/or future plans. If the interviewee is planning to build a career in that industry, the employer may be comforted since it could mean they are more likely to stay in the position. If the interviewee is unsure, the employer could be leery of their commitment to the job.

How to respond: Your response to this question should include information that's beyond the job description and include your interests in the industry as a whole. Say what brought you into the field and what you think your career will look like. Be sure to tell the interviewer how their position would help you along your career journey within your chosen field. (Good think you just thought about this!)

How to screw this up: If you're unable to convey your interests beyond the job, it could hinder your chances at getting it. As I stated above, the employer might feel like you're a flight risk and not hire you because they don't want to go through the same process a few months down the road. If you're genuinely not interested in the field but still want the job, be honest. Convince your interviewers that the job itself is something that you can see yourself doing for the long haul

What is your ideal job or work situation?

This question requires you to think about your work style and the conditions under which you are most successful. Interviewers ask this type of question as a way to gauge your fit with the environment in their organization or department. If your responds runs askew of how they operate day-to-day, it could indicate to the employer that you won't be satisfied in the job (even if you're good at it).

How to respond: Be honest but strategic. Use your research to get an idea of how the department works, and highlight the places that you think your work style aligns with their environment. If you can't find this information, then go with your gut. Say the things that would be deal-breakers for your professional success and satisfaction, and see where it takes you.

How to screw this up: Knowing how their company works and deliberately giving work conditions that run counter to it is really the only way to mess up this question. You have to highlight points of compromise or else you're wasting everyone's time in this interview, including your own. Remember: If they don't operate in a way that will allow you to be successful, then this probably isn't the job for you.

_____

_____

_____

_____

_____

_____

_____

_____

_____
_____
_____
_____
_____
_____
_____
_____
_____
_____
_____
_____
_____
_____
_____
_____
_____

Where do you think you can add value to the organization?
Employers always want to feel like they're getting a deal, so they prefer candidates that have skill sets beyond what is outlined in the job description. As the interviewee, it is your responsibility to highlight both your qualifications for the role and the relevant skills you have that can allow you to contribute in ways that other candidates may not. Even though they want people with more, the interviewers may not specifically ask about it, so you need to be ready to supply your extra skills whenever possible.

How to respond: Your research on both the job and the

company will come in handy here, as you will know what skills the interviewer will value the most. Lay it on thick and discuss specific initiatives and/or projects where your skill set would come in handy. Technology and social media skills are great go-to answers for this (unless you're going for a job in tech or social media!) because there is always some program or software that can make projects easier, yet isn't used by technophobes.

How to screw this up: You have to walk the line between "add value" and "fix problems", as the employer may have a different idea of what issues they have. If you go in talking about how your skills can solve things that they don't see as problems, the interviewer may feel slighted (even if you're correct). Framing is the key to ensuring that you're not being offensive.

If you were not extended an offer, why do you think that would be?

This question requires you to discuss the shortcomings of your application. Unlike a question like 'What is your greatest weakness', you don't have to point out a specific flaw or discuss how you're looking to shore up any issues that you may recognize in yourself. Rather, you have to provide the interviewers with the way that you would justify not being hired. It is a wordy way to ask, "Why wouldn't we hire you?"

How to respond: This is another one where you need to be honest but strategic in answering this question, as it is very easy to harp on the negatives. Instead of just pointing out a specific area where you are lacking, put the onus on the interviewers to see things from your perspective.

For example: If the job wants 5 years of experience and you only have 3, bring this up in a way that shows that *you* don't think it will be an issue if hired for the job. Something like "You may not hire me because I was unable to convey that, despite my lack of direct experience, I can still do this job very well" is a great way to convey your confidence in yourself.

How to screw this up: Saying "I don't know" or something along the lines of "You're dumb" are the exact wrong ways to answer this question. You have to show that you're self-aware enough to know that you're not the perfect candidate (because this person does not exist), but also show that you believe in yourself and your qualifications for the job.

_____
_____
_____
_____
_____
_____
_____
_____
_____
_____
_____
_____
_____
_____
_____
_____
_____
_____
_____
_____
_____
_____
_____
_____
_____
_____
_____
_____

If you didn't have to work, what would you do with your time?

Questions about time spent out-of-work are ways that interviewers can get a better sense of who you are as a person. How you would spend your time if employment were not a necessity gives them an idea of your priorities, likes, and values. It is unlikely that employment decisions will be based on this information, but your responses could color the way your interviewers see you.

How to respond: Your response to this question could reveal information that is illegal for interviewers to ask, so be careful in how you respond. If you're concerned that revealing your religion or culture could negatively impact your employment prospects, then steer clear of any answer that could reveal these things. Likewise, if you believe that your status as a parent or spouse could be red flags, don't bring up your family. The safe way to answer this question is with an innocuous hobby or random dream career.

How to screw this up: This one is pretty open, so it would be tough to mess up. As long as you steer clear of illegal activities or things that run directly counter the job you're interviewing for, you should be okay.

What resources do you use to stay on top of industry trends?

If you're using your own time to remain current with the trends of your industry, it is clear that you're invested in developing a career. This will show the interviewer that you're in it for the long haul, which is definitely a good thing. As stated a few times above, commitment to the field illustrates to the employer that you want their job for the right reasons.

How to respond: The answer to this question is pretty straightforward: Just say whatever resources you use to stay current on the field. These could be keyword specific Google alerts, newspapers, books, blogs, LinkedIn influencers, etc., whatever you use, say it. List out the resources along with the frequency with which you access them.

How to screw this up: The most obvious way to mess up is to not be current on industry trends. For the host of reasons outlined above, you should start this practice ASAP. Aside from this, if you say you use a resource but can't discuss anything from it, then you'll look like a liar. For example: If you say you read *The Economist* but don't know what was in their most recent issue, the interviewer won't believe that you actually read *The Economist*. Even if you do, don't list out resources that you can't speak intelligently about.

CHAPTER 7
ILLEGAL INTERVIEW TOPICS

In this chapter, we will go over what information is illegal for an interviewer to ask and what the questions could look like in an interview. The activity for this chapter will help you with how to decide if disclosing this information is the right thing for you to do by brainstorming the pros and cons of sharing with a potential employer.

Note: This is very United States-centric information because of the distinct laws and legal history of my country. If you're concerned about what an interviewer can and cannot ask in your country, definitely do your research. There are similar protections outside of the USofA, but I don't know enough about the specifics.

Interviewing is often compared to an interrogation because the interviewer's job is to probe for information. They ask a bunch of questions in order to find out everything they can about their interviewee so that they can then make the right hiring decision. While there is nothing wrong with this, there are some interviewers that will try to gather information that is illegal to ask because of the potential to impact the interviewee's chances of getting the job.

As you'll see below, the key point that makes these topics off limits is that they have nothing to do with an applicant's ability to do the job. Rather, they're personal details that could be deemed either positive or negative based on the whims of a particular employer.

Even though it is illegal for interviewers to ask for the information described below, it is ultimately up to you to decide if you want to disclose things on your own. If you find yourself in a situation where the best answer to the interviewer's question involves sharing, then it may work in your favor to do so.

A few examples: If you're actively involved in professional organizations related to a particular affinity group, then it could be useful to discuss your experiences with them. Or if you're a mom who is looking to reenter the workforce after raising kids, then talking about your parental status is inevitable since it explains your employment gap. Or if you're applying to be a translator and your proficiency with the language is based on your country of origin, then it would probably help you to say that in your interview.

As long as you're comfortable with the interviewer having personal information beyond what they are able to ask, then say what you feel is right. If you're at all unsure of how this information will be used, however, then it is probably best to keep it to yourself.

The section below provides details on some of the main categories of illegal information. In the space provided after each topic area, brainstorm the pros and cons of sharing this information with a potential employer.

Race and Ethnicity

Information regarding race and ethnicity is illegal because of the history of racism and racially discriminatory hiring practices. Until the Civil Rights Act of 1964 created the Equal Employment Opportunity Commission (EEOC), employers regularly passed over qualified applicants because of their race or ethnicity. There are stories of lighter-skinned people of color who would pass for white to get better jobs. (Some members of my family were part of this group.) While times have changed since the passage of this legislation, and being a person a color won't automatically exclude you from a position, there is still evidence of discrimination in hiring.

Since race and ethnicity can sometimes be visibly assessed for (maybe not accurately, but it's still clear when an interviewee isn't white), interviewers typically don't ask questions about it. Also, since they're some of the more obviously illegal pieces of information, many interviewers avoid discussion of them altogether.

What are the pros of sharing this information in an interview?

___

What are the cons?

Brainstorm specific circumstances where you would volunteer this information.

_____
_____
_____
_____
_____
_____
_____
_____
_____
_____
_____

Gender Identity and Sexual Orientation

Similar to race and ethnicity, gender identity and sexual orientation are covered through the Civil Rights Act of 1964, though they were added much later. This information is illegal because, similar to race and ethnicity, there is a history of employment discrimination related to gender identity and sexual orientation. Unlike race and ethnicity, however, there are still places where this type of exclusionary behavior is okay – and even applauded. The recent spate of anti-transgender rulings is clear evidence of this. As of 2015, only 22 states and the District of Columbia had specific rules about employment discrimination based on gender identity and sexual orientation.

Questions that could try to gather this information in a round-about way would be ones that focused on your outside of work activities. For example, an interviewer asking things like "What professional organizations do you belong to" or "How do you spend your free time" could lead an unprepared interviewee to disclose such information.

What are the pros of sharing this information in an interview?

_____
_____
_____
_____
_____
_____
_____
_____
_____
_____

What are the cons?

_____
_____
_____
_____
_____
_____
_____
_____
_____
_____

Brainstorm specific circumstances where you would volunteer this information.

_____
_____
_____
_____
_____
_____
_____
_____
_____
_____

Marital and/or Parental Status

An employer would be interested in your marital and/or parental status because it could factor into how much time you would need to take off for various family-related events or give insights into your general lifestyle. A few examples: If you're a newlywed (or engaged) woman, the employer could assume that you'll soon be starting a family and not want to deal with a new employee on maternity leave. If you're a mom with kids the employer could assume that you're going to be in and out of the office for school-related events. If you're not married, the employer could make assumptions of your sexual orientation or general lifestyle that run counter to their beliefs. The key to all of this is negative employer assumptions. This information is illegal in an interview because it has nothing to do with your ability to do a job, and everything to do with the employer potentially judging you based on your personal life.

An interviewer who is trying to discover this information could ask you directly about your family situation (rare), or inquire about "responsibilities" that could take you away from work.

What are the pros of sharing this information in an interview?

_____
_____
_____
_____
_____
_____
_____
_____
_____
_____

What are the cons?

_____
_____
_____
_____
_____
_____
_____
_____
_____
_____

Brainstorm specific circumstances where you would volunteer this information.

_____
_____
_____
_____
_____
_____
_____
_____
_____
_____

Ability Status

The American with Disabilities Act (ADA) of 1990 made it illegal for a potential employer to discriminate against applicants based on their ability status. While the individual can't have a disability or disorder that is a major function of the job, the employer cannot exclude someone from their applicant pool because they do not want to provide the "reasonable accommodations" that are required by this law. This hold true for both physical and mental disabilities, though the former are typically easier for the interviewer to discern.

Curiosity about mental ability is often satisfied by past performance in academic settings or in similar jobs. Unfortunately, assumptions about mental dis/abilities are often tied to stereotypes that surround an individual's specific group (usually racial or ethnic), so this could potentially be doubly oppressive to an interviewee whose interviewer holds such prejudices.

Inquiries about ability status could revolve around accommodations or health. Be wary of how you answer questions like "What would we need to give you in order for you to be successful in this position" and "Are there any physical reasons that would make you unable to perform specific aspects of this job."

What are the pros of sharing this information in an interview?

___
___
___
___
___
___
___
___
___
___

What are the cons?

___
___
___
___
___
___

Brainstorm specific circumstances where you would volunteer this information.

Age

It is illegal for an interviewer to ask a candidate's age because this information has nothing to do with whether or not they are qualified for a position. In the vast majority of fields, there isn't an age limit on the ability to acquire skills or perform them at a high level. But age discrimination is very real.

Individuals who are over 40 face a difficult time on the job market because employers 1) believe that they won't be in the workforce for much long and don't want to waste resources on them, 2) don't think they are technologically experienced enough to handle the demands of today's workplace, and 3) don't want to pay them at a rate commensurate to their experience. As the economy recovered from the Great Recession, for example, laid-off individuals from this group faced tremendous challenges with regaining employment because of these assumptions. Many of them were forced to take positions that were lower than the ones they separated from or completely changed fields because they needed to find an income.

Indirect ways that interviewers could try to determine your age is to ask about graduation dates or bring up generational or cultural markers that could reveal such information.

What are the pros of sharing this information in an interview?

_____
_____
_____
_____
_____
_____
_____
_____
_____

What are the cons?

_____
_____
_____

Brainstorm specific circumstances where you would volunteer this information.

Religion

An interviewer would be interested in an interviewee's religion for both personal and professional reasons. On the personal side, they might share a common faith and be able to build rapport over it. On the professional, they may want to know if you'd be taking time off to observe religious holidays. While these are seemingly legitimate reasons to get this information, it's illegal to ask about religion in an interview because it doesn't have a bearing on how the applicant will do in the job. Most importantly, an applicant's lack of religion or belief in a faith that runs counter to the interviewer's beliefs could have an negative impact on their job prospects, even if they are otherwise qualified for the position.

Interviewers who are curious about your religious affiliation could ask about holidays or outside of work activities as ways to get this information. I've also seen some directly ask about membership to a specific religious institution, but this is rare.

What are the pros of sharing this information in an interview?

What are the cons?

_____

Brainstorm specific circumstances where you would volunteer this information.

_____

National Origin and/or Citizenship Status

While certain employers will need this information in the hiring process – like the federal government, organizations that deal directly with them, or if they'll have to attempt to get sponsorship – in general, asking interviewees about their nationality and/or citizenship status is illegal. The reason is one that should be familiar to you at this point of the chapter: stereotypes, assumptions, and discrimination.

In terms of nationality, an interviewer could have negative views of a country or region based on world events or personal perception. With citizenship status, and interviewer could force an undocumented immigrant to disclose this status, which would have implications far beyond employment. It is okay if the interviewer asks about the interviewee's work authorization, however, because it doesn't automatically belie citizenship. Undocumented individuals with deferred action status, for example, are able to work legally in the United States despite their status.

There aren't very many covert ways to gather nationality or citizenship information, so expect these to be more direct, especially if you have an accent or non-Anglo name.

What are the pros of sharing this information in an interview?

_____
_____
_____
_____
_____
_____
_____
_____
_____
_____
_____

What are the cons?

_____
_____

_____
_____
_____
_____
_____
_____
_____
_____
_____
_____

Brainstorm specific circumstances where you would volunteer this information.

_____
_____
_____
_____
_____
_____
_____
_____

Substance use/abuse history

Since addiction is a disability covered under the ADA, asking about past substance use and abuse is illegal. While it is inadvisable for a recovering addict to work with or around the substance they were addicted to, it is not legal for an employment decision to be based on the applicant's medical history. Questions surrounding this are rare, but if you fall into this category keep your rights in mind.

What are the pros of sharing this information in an interview?

___

What are the cons?

___

Brainstorm specific circumstances where you would volunteer this information.

_____
_____
_____
_____
_____
_____
_____
_____
_____
_____

Key Take-Away Points

- Certain information is illegal in an interview because it can unduly sway the interviewer's opinions of the interviewee based on personal factors that have no bearing on the individual's ability to perform the functions of the job.
- Be wary of questions that ask about outside of work activities and responsibilities, as they could be attempts to gather such information in an indirect way.
- You don't have to answer any question – illegal or otherwise – that makes you feel uncomfortable. If you get such inquiries in an interview, you should question whether or not that organization is a good place for you to be.

CHAPTER 8
NONVERBAL COMMUNICATION & PROFESSIONAL PRESENTATION

In this chapter, we'll go into the ways that you can say a lot with out saying a word.

The old saying "Action speak louder than words" proves true for interviewing, as your nonverbal communication during an interview is just as important as your verbal responses to the questions. You can say all the 'right' things and be highly qualified for the position, but if you don't *seem* like you want it then your chances of getting an offer are slim.

So how do you *seem* like you want the job? Here are four ways.

Be enthusiastic for the position.

The purpose of the interview is to convince someone to hire you, but nobody wants to hire a candidate who doesn't convey that they want the job they're interviewing for. Being sullen or matter-of-fact about the position could come across as you not really wanting to do it, even if that's not true. Just because you took the time to apply doesn't mean your job is done. You need to sell your interest for the position.

The easiest way to show enthusiasm is to smile. Smile in appropriate places when you talk about your experiences and tell your stories. Pep up your demeanor when answering questions by being expressive with your eyes and tone. (This advice is helpful even if you're on a phone interview because when you smile your voice changes.) If you find yourself doing an impression of April Ludgate or Daria Morgendorffer, then you're doing it wrong.

This may seem of feel disingenuous if you're an introvert or naturally reserved, but you have to amp-up your personality in interview settings because that's what gets you hired. I'm not saying that you should become a bubbly ball of pep for the sake of employment! But if your natural energy level is at a 3, try to bump it up to a 6. Use your nerves to give you the energy you may not normally have. As long as your responses are authentic and real, then you aren't being disingenuous. You're just playing the game.

Make eye contact with your interviewers.

I can't count on my fingers and toes how many times I've done mock interviews where the participant spoke more to the floor or their shoulder than they did to me. Eye contact is one of the most important nonverbal skills for having a successful interview because it conveys confidence and self-assuredness. These soft skills are critical for workplace success in the vast majority of industries, and the only way an employer will know that you have them is if you show them in your interview.

Your eye contact must be natural, or else you'll look like a creep. Don't stare down your interviewer! It's okay to look away sometimes while your thinking, and be sure to blink in natural intervals. If there is more than one person interviewing you (which is very common), then be sure to engage each one by looking around the room while you're responding. Meeting eyes with everyone is a great way to acknowledge their presence.

Note: Making eye contact with people in positions of power is a distinctly Western convention, so if you're not in the United States or Europe then this advice may not be the best route to take in an interview. In some cultures, this is extremely disrespectful and could cost you the job. When in doubt, do what is culturally appropriate for your location and audience.

Take notes during the interview.

In addition to your resume, cover letter, and list of questions for the interviewer, you should always bring a pen and a pad of paper to an interview. Use these tools to take notes throughout the meeting. If the interviewers say something interesting or ask you a question that you've never encountered, write it down. You can use this information for the thank you notes you'll have to write post-interview, and also for your own professional development.

Taking notes is also a great way to show that you're paying attention (or force yourself to pay attention if your interviewer is particularly long winded). Even if you have a great memory and know that you'll be able to recall the conversation, remember that the interviewer doesn't know this about you. Writing things down makes it clear that you're in it to win it.

Dress for interview success.

On top of this in-interview behavior, you also need to dress the part. Now, I'm not one to ever tell folks how to dress. (I consciously don't write blog posts about it.) I'm a firm believer in production over packaging when you're at work, so I'm not the one to come to for fashion advice. The key phrase of that last sentence, however, is "when you're at work." If you already have the job, your presentation doesn't matter nearly as much as it does when you're interviewing.

So how should you make your sartorial decisions come interview day? Use your research! Figure out the standard dress code for your industry and go one step above the position you're interviewing for. Don't wear what the people in the job wear since you're not in it yet. If you're interviewing to be an auto mechanic, don't show up in an oily jumpsuit! Khakis and a button up shirt are fine. "Professional" means different things for different positions and industries, so you shouldn't default to a suit.

Other appearance considerations

In addition to clothing, hair, makeup, and scents should also be taken into consideration. Scent is easy - don't wear perfume or use heavily perfumed products prior to an interview. If your interviewer is sensitive to smells or if you accidentally use too much, it could be distracting and off-putting to the people you're meeting with. For makeup, use the same rules you went by when deciding what to wear. Unless you're interviewing for a position where your appearance is part of the job description, you should err to the side of natural.

Hair is a tricky one since it can be seen as a political statement. This is especially true for women of color, since our hair has historically been used as a tool of our oppression. Certain textures have been deemed unprofessional, thus mandating women to damage our hair to make it more acceptable or risk not being able to work. While such explicit rules are slowly being relaxed (pun kind of intended), they are still in place. In 2016, a court ruled that employers can legally deny jobs to people with dreadlocks, which is a hairstyle that is indicative of the African diaspora.

While research can inform your hairstyling choices, keep it within reason. Don't shave your dreadlocks or chemically change your hair because an employer may not like it. If they don't, then is that really a company you want to work for? Make that decision for yourself.

NOW PRACTICE!

This chapter's exercise is one of my favorites. First, you'll need to go back to the previous exercises and pull up your responses to the prompts. Then, you have to pick a few questions and video record yourself answering them with your prepared answers. Once you're done, watch the video and use the mock interview rubric to score yourself. Repeat this process until you are satisfied with your performance.

I love this activity because it both helps you practice and helps you get an idea of how you come across in an interview. Having a third-person view of yourself is immensely useful. If you don't like what you see, then you have a chance to change it *before* it costs you a job!

MOCK INTERVIEW SELF-CRITIQUE RUBRIC

Content of response

Clarity

3 – Responses were clear stories with well-defined talking points, and the examples made sense to the questions that were asked.

2 – Responses were clear in some places but not all. Talking points were ambiguous with some examples making more sense to the questions that were asked than others.

1 – Responses were ambiguous and tangential. Talking points were unclear and did not answer the questions that were asked.

Your score: _____

Notes

_____
_____
_____
_____
_____
_____
_____
_____
_____
_____

Precision

3 – Responses were concise and to the point, and thoroughly answered the questions.

2 – Responses had a few places of unnecessary content and extra examples, but ultimately answered the questions.

1 – Responses too awhile to get to actually answering the question, if they did so at all.

Your score: _____

Notes

_____
_____
_____
_____
_____
_____
_____
_____
_____

Linear Progression

3 – Responses moved along in an order that made sense, and had a clear flow and narrative arc.

2 – Responses were stilted at times but generally made sense and flowed well enough to understand the overall point.

1 – Responses were difficult to follow and did not make sense.

Your score: _____

Notes

_____
_____
_____
_____
_____

Delivery of response

Verbal Articulation

3 – You fully formed your words and were easy to understand at all times.

2 – Your speech was a bit garbled or muffled at times, but overall you could be understood.

1 – You were inaudible and/or incoherent for a majority of your responses.

Your score: _____

Notes

Word Choice

3 – All of your words were appropriate and standard for both the industry you are interviewing for and the language that is common between you and your interviewer.

2 – Most of your words were appropriate and standard, but some were too colloquial for an interview.

1 – The majority of your words were inappropriate, nonstandard, and too colloquial for an interview.

Your score: _____

Notes

_____
_____
_____
_____
_____
_____
_____
_____
_____

Enthusiasm For The Position

3 – Both your words and your body language showed that you wanted the job,

2 – Either your words or your body language showed that you

wanted the job.

1 – Neither your words nor your body language showed that you wanted the job.

Your score: _____

Notes

_____
_____
_____
_____
_____
_____
_____
_____
_____

Nonverbal communication

Eye Contact

3 – You maintained steady, natural eye contact throughout the interview

2 – You had minimal and/or unnatural eye contact throughout the interview.

1 – You were on the extremes: either no eye contact or far too much.

Your score: _____

Notes

_____
_____
_____
_____
_____
_____
_____
_____
_____

General Body Language

3 – You had an open, easy, relaxed posture throughout the interview.

2 – You had an open, easy posture for part of the interview, but appeared closed and/or distracted at some points.

1 – You appeared closed and/or distracted throughout the interview.

Your score: _____

Notes

_____
_____

_____
_____
_____
_____
_____
_____
_____
_____

Facial Expression

3 – Your facial expressions were appropriate for their associated responses, and you appeared engaged throughout the interview.

2 – Your facial expression was the same throughout the interview, not matter the response you were giving.

1 – Your facial expression appeared angry, frustrated, and/or defeated throughout the interview.

Your score: _____

Notes

_____
_____
_____
_____
_____
_____
_____

_____
_____
_____
_____

Reflection
_____

What else did you notice about yourself in the video?

_____
_____
_____
_____
_____
_____
_____
_____
_____
_____

List and describe three things you did well.

_____
_____
_____
_____
_____
_____
_____

_____

List and describe three things you want to work on.

_____

Which story worked best? Why?

_____

Which story do you need to fix? How will you do this?

CHAPTER 9
INTERACTING WITH INTERVIEWERS

In the previous chapter, we discussed the part of interviewing success that goes beyond answering questions. Your nonverbal communication is critical, but so are the ways that you interact with interviewers both during and after the interview. In this one, we'll talk about asking your interviewer questions and the best ways to thank them afterwards. These are two areas that many interviewees fall short.

Asking Questions

At the end of every interview, the interviewer will ask you if you have any questions for them. You always should. Why? It shows that you're using the interview for what it really is: a learning opportunity. You can't possibly have learned everything about the company from researching their website and reading the news, and they know this. Asking questions shows that you want to make an informed decision about where to spend the next few years of your life, and highlights the level of seriousness with which you are taking the recruiting process.

You should have 10 questions prepared for every interview, but know that you'll probably have time to only ask 5-7 of them. Write them down (or type them out) and bring the list with you. This is a good strategy for two reasons.

1) Having a physical list helps you remember your questions. Interviews are long and stressful, so you can't count on your brain to recall everything that you want to know once the interviewers turn the meeting over to you. Having a physical list of questions is one less thing you need to

worry about remembering.

2) If during the course of the interview the questions are answered, your list will show the interviewers that you had prepared for this aspect of the interview. If you just say "You answered all of my questions" without proof that you had them, your interviewers may not believe you. If end up in a situation where your questions have been covered, you can ask the interviewers to elaborate on the questions that you feel are most important, prefacing your inquiries with "You touched on this before, but can you say more about..." This phrasing shows that you were paying attention.

Your questions should be a mix of information gathering about both the position and the company, and should not be about things that are easy to find on their website. When coming up with questions, think about your deal-breakers: What would you absolutely need to be successful in this job at this company? Once you have them, use them to formulate your questions. Good places to start are with company culture, growth potential, opportunities for advancement, professional development, and the interviewers' opinions of and experiences with the company.

This is not the place to ask about compensation or benefits. Bringing up money and perks can imply to the interviewer that you're more interested in that aspect of the job than the job itself. While the former are important to most people, let the interviewers bring up this part. It's just a much better look for you if you're more focused on the job itself.

Thank You Notes

Always send your interviewers thank you notes within 24-48 hours of the interview. To ensure that your interviewer receives the note in a timely fashion, you should email it as opposed to sending it by post. Be sure to send a personalized one to every person in your interview, not just the one who set it up. This can be time consuming if you met with multiple people (or groups), but it is useful in maintaining a positive impression with the decision-makers.

Thank you notes are useful because they help you stand out from the crowd. Even though they are proper interviewing etiquette, not everyone writes them. (A recruiter once told me that only about 10-15% of their interviewees reach out afterwards.) Yours will put you in a positive light just by doing one. And, if an interviewer is doing multiple interviews for a single position, this note can remind them of who you are and what you discussed. This information may come into play during the final hiring decision.

These notes don't have to be long or fancy. A 3-5 sentence email thanking the individual for their time, commenting on something you learned or appreciated, and reiterating your interest in the position is all you have to do. It can be longer if you feel the need to ask more questions or want to clarify something from the interview - which are definitely okay. While this gesture may seem minor, I have seen the lack of a thank you note make candidates go from the "maybe" pile to a firm "no."

NOW PRACTICE!

Use the space provided to come up with questions for a potential interviewer. Follow the directions on the worksheet and use a job description that is close to what you'd ultimately like to do.

CREATE YOUR QUESTIONS

Review your notes about the company and job, and write out five to seven questions that you could ask your interviewers.

CHAPTER 10
WELLNESS CHECK

Looking for work (even if you're currently employed) is stressful, and the longer it goes the more demoralizing it becomes. Sending out countless applications and getting rejections (or no response at all) is mentally and physically exhausting. You start to question yourself, your qualifications, and even your worthiness to do the job that you want. If you're feeling defeated, and this sense of defeat bleeds into the interview, then it becomes even more likely that you won't get the job. It's hard to convey enthusiasm when you're beat down.

But you have to maintain a positive outlook on your job search for there to be a positive result. You have to know that this is just temporary and that you'll be better for it, or else things can get unhealthily bleak. The job search is the type of thing that sucks until it doesn't. It's going to be awful until you have a new job, so keep that in mind. It's not easy, but it'll be worth it.

If you're at the breaking point, you need to be proactive in ensuring that your stress doesn't impact your interview performance. I've met some people can just flip a switch and go into the interview all sunshine and lollipops, ready to go no matter what the external circumstances are. If you're one of those people who can fake it 'til they make it, good for you! Use this trait to exude positivity in every interview.

If you can't - and that's totally okay - you need to be more deliberate about it. You need to actively invoke a positive attitude by any means necessary. Here are three quick ways to do that.

1. Be nice to yourself.

In the time leading up to the interview (and always, really), be kind to yourself. Cook yourself a nice meal. Get your nails done. Go to the movies. Take a nap. (My personal favorite!) Do whatever you need to do to make yourself relaxed. These sorts of activities serve to de-stress the body and mind, and put you in a better mental space to rock the interview. Pump yourself up when you do something good, no matter how small. If you make a mistake, don't beat yourself up. Laugh about it. Keep things light and positive, and deflect the negativity and stress.

2. Acknowledge your situation.

Stress and anxiety become compounded and exacerbated when we don't allow for them in our lives. When we try too hard to push through as if everything is fine, we make things worse. Instead of ignoring your situation, allow yourself to acknowledge it. If you find yourself feeling down about a rejection letter or an unsuccessful interview, sit with it for a bit. Let yourself grieve for an option that has been lost and reflect on what you could have done differently in that situation. Set a time limit for this, then take the steps to move on once the time is up. This simple activity will help you be able to close the loop on crappy experiences more quickly so that they don't get you down in the long term.

3. Create some portable inspiration.

Inspirational quotes and phrases are helpful in maintaining sanity because they're a quick and easy way to keep yourself going. Many of us have vision boards (or Pinterest boards) that are explicitly for this purpose, and if you don't I encourage you to make one. You never know when you'll need it! In addition to these static or virtual options, you should have ones that you can pull up at any time. When you find quotes that resonate with you, write them on a physical piece of paper. Keep the list in your purse or wallet and post the mantras around your house. Look at them whenever you need to!

FINAL THOUGHTS

Interviewing is tough and very subjective, but preparation is helpful in ensuring that you did everything you could to get the job. Now that you have the process down, keep at it! Get in the habit of assessing yourself and reflecting on what you've done. Stay in the know about companies and industries you're interested in. Work on the practice questions with friends and family. Use the self-critique rubric to assess yourself and your progress. Be as polished as possible in your interview to remove any doubt in the interviewer's mind that you are the right person for the job.

Remember: The interviewers already like you! Now go out and get hired.

ABOUT THE AUTHOR

Lindsay R. Granger, EdD is a higher education professional and private career success coach who writes about career preparation and success on her website: lindsaygranger.com. She has worked in the future-focused counseling space for the past decade, at both secondary and postsecondary levels. In recent years, Lindsay has both worked as a career advisor and studied career readiness strategies for underserved populations.

www.ingramcontent.com/pod-product-compliance
Lightning Source LLC
Chambersburg PA
CBHW071444180526
45170CB00001B/456